LEADING

SERVICE BEFORE SELF

My Personal Journey

JOHN M. LOTZ

Brigadier General, USAF, Retired

PANGÆA
Publishing Group

LEADING: SERVICE BEFORE SELF

ISBN 978-1-950134-59-5
Pangæa Publishing Group
www.PangaeaPublishing.com

Cover images:

United States Air Force logo and rank insignia
Public domain, via Wikimedia Commons
USA flag by Wagner France 3D @ Freepik.com
Square abstract frame by Rawpixel.com @ Freepik.com

Fleurons @ Freepik.com
Divisors @ Freepik.com

Cover design and typesetting by
DesignPeaks@gmail.com

DESIGN PEAKS®

For information contact:

PANGÆA PUBLISHING GROUP
25579 Carmel Knolls Drive, Carmel, CA 93923 – USA
Telephone: 831-649-0669 – Email: info@pangaeapublishing.com

Dedication

To My Family:

… devoted to one another in love …
(Romans 12:10).

To Veterans and Their Families:

"Greater love has no one than this:
to lay down one's life for one's friends" (John 15:13).

To My Family

Margaret Bryan Lotz, high school sweetheart, fiancé and wife. Sixty-three years wedded. To our life together as we matured as children, young adults and as a couple. The child we created and the grandchildren she blessed us with.

Our daughter, Laura Murcott. "Squirt." An easy child to raise. The special father-daughter relationship. The special mother-daughter relationship. Air Force C-130 Navigator and Combat Veteran. Mother to our three grandchildren:

Drew Murcott. Our war baby. Born in 2003. Mom left for the Iraqi theater in the Spring of 2004. Taking care of Drew while she was away. What a blessing. Quiet. Good heart. Smart. Likes technology and building.

Alexis Murcott. The older of the familial twins (by three minutes). Outgoing. Savy. Athletic.

Torrey Murcott. The "younger," according to her sister. Bright. Artistic. A critical thinker. Giving.

There is no way to describe what family means to us and how much we love them and each other.

To Our Veterans and Their Families

September 11, 2022

Today we salute those who served in the military and their families. They are a very special group of people. Those who have not served, generally understand the horrific nature of war and the wounds of war, physical and mental, suffered by veterans and their families. I thank all of you for that understanding and appreciation.

However, veterans and their families sacrifice so much more. The short list includes: lower incomes that have forced younger members to enroll for welfare assistance; emotional trauma for families when their vet has to deploy-the pall of death; and frequent moves that hit the children the hardest. But you understand these sacrifices and give credit.

The impact of social unrest on our military, however, is unspoken. I joined as a teenager in 1959. The Vietnam War was ramping up and the United Sates sent combat units to Vietnam starting in 1965. Social unrest swept through our country in the decade of the '60s: The Vietnam War, the Civil Rights Movement and the "hippie, Summer of Love" movement.

A large part of our society in the decade of the '60s vented their disapproval of the Vietnam War directly on military members and their families. In uniform, we were often jeered or spat at. The press could not get beyond fraggings and drug use in Vietnam. Small businesses denied military members credit.

Under McNamara, the military lost its roots in leadership. Discipline disintegrated. Millions died, civilian and military. Imagine a military member fighting for his or her country without the support of its citizens. Disagreeing with policy is far different than taking those policies out on the men and women we ordered (the draft) to serve.

Here, again, our men and women and families took it on the chin for us. We failed, as a society, to protect them. The military did not fully recover from these depredations and disruptions until the mid-eighties. But now, societal changes are negatively affecting our military once again.

The draft is gone. There will be a breaking point again. I thank all of you who have served and are serving. We ask so much of you and your families.

JOHN M. LOTZ
BRIG. GEN., USAF, RETIRED

TABLE OF CONTENTS

FORWARD

"To aspire to leadership is an honorable ambition"
(1 Timothy 3:1).

"The greatest among you shall be your servant" (Mathew 23:11).

"Be completely humble and gentle; be patient,
bearing with one another in love" (Ephesians 4:2).

Mason Williams, who wrote "Classical Gas," put this ditty to song: "Isn't life beautiful, isn't life gay, isn't life the perfect thing to pass the time away."

The core to effective leadership is serving others, and I have found that this attitude is uplifting and yields positive returns for those led and those leading. It is a team sport. Let serving others help make your "life the perfect thing to pass the time away."

It is likely that most people will lead in some capacity during their lifetime. My journey as a leader was molded by my upbringing, the influence of individual role models, historical events and by making many mistakes along the way.

As a young man, my parents taught me disciplines that would help me to be a leader. Later, I was deeply influenced by three major historical events: the "Summer of Love" as I call the hippie movement starting in the late '50s; the Vietnam War; and the Civil Rights movement. These events were rife with lessons about leadership regardless of where you stood politically.

Another formative force were the leaders I worked for, a story that kept unfolding for the rest of my career. Finally, it all comes together as you lead and get "on the job training," i.e., learning by trial and error.

My goal is to encourage you to become a leader, purposefully. To Serve and to Unite people. However, you will encounter constraints.

"The true measure of leadership is influence, nothing more, nothing less."[1] A leader needs to gain influence in order to carry out

1. *"21 Laws of Leadership in the Bible," John C. Maxwell, 2018.*

the goals of the organization that he or she leads. The pathway to influence is discussed in the Chapter "One Man's Journey."

Individually, we live and lead for a very short time. We hope that we will have been an example to those we lead. We hope our efforts bear fruit and that we leave "the campsite better than we found it."

We retire and reflect. I have no illusion that any success I may have in life will change human nature at its core, or that I have weakened Evil at its core. Instead, I find that:

1. *As you age, there is a natural, but I believe informed, pessimism that grows in your soul. At the end of his life, King Solomon said:*

   "What has been is what will be, and what has been done is what will be done, and there is nothing new under the sun" (Ecclesiastes 1:9).

2. *Evil does exist. There is a biblical battle between good and evil that is described in the Scriptures. People cross the line between good and evil daily.*

   "If only there were evil people somewhere insidiously committing evil deeds, and it were necessary only to separate them from the rest of us and destroy them. But the line dividing good and evil cuts through the heart of every human being. And who is willing to destroy a piece of his own heart?" [2]

3. *Because human nature is static, each generation "relives" the past creating continual cycles such as the life of nations:*

---

2. *"Gulag Archipelago," Aleksandr Solzhenitsyn, 1962.*

"A democracy is always temporary in nature; it simply cannot exist as a permanent form of government. A democracy will continue to exist up until the time that voters discover that they can vote themselves generous gifts from the public treasury. From that moment on, the majority always votes for the candidates who promise the most benefits from the public treasury, with the results that every democracy will finally collapse over loose fiscal policy, (which is) always followed by a dictatorship."

The average age of the world's greatest civilizations from the beginning of history, has been 200 years. During those 200 years, these nations always progressed through the following sequence:

- *From bondage to spiritual faith;*
- *From spiritual faith to great courage;*
- *From courage to liberty;*
- *From liberty to abundance;*
- *From abundance to complacency;*
- *From complacency to apathy;*
- *From apathy to dependence;*
- *From dependence back into bondage.*[3]

---

3. *Alexander Tyler, 1887, Scottish Professor of History, University of Edinburgh, RE: the fall of the Athenian Republic.*

In Summary

This may not be a cheery prologue. Every generation virtually starts over again. The need to "raise" new leaders occurs in every generation. Our country's pathway is suggested by Alexander Tyler in the words above. Thomas Jefferson also warns us about the diligence necessary to maintain our liberties (Pg. 91).

Our lifetime privilege is to serve others. At its core, the leader is a mentor and a role model. As you learn and grow, pass it on. You may not move the master dials that change human nature, but you can improve lives and motivate those you lead during your "threescore and ten years" (70 years) of life on this earth.

The ability to lead is not conveyed by title, position, or organizational authority. Leading is an unending process of self-discovery and adaptation to events confronting you as you learn how to be more influential. Biblically, the expectations of a leader are high:

> *"Be shepherds of God's flock that is under your care, watching over them-not because you must, but because you are willing, as God wants you to be; not pursuing dishonest gain, but eager to serve; not for personal gain, but being [an] example[s]..." (Peter 5:2).*

Today this country needs an abundance of principled leaders willing to serve.

LIVING THE AMERICAN DREAM

"And though your beginning was small,
your latter days will be very great" (Job 8:7).

My story begins with "privilege." I had no father to guide me. My mother, a divorcee, raised us and insured we had those privileges. Those privileges are now derogatorily called "white privileges." We called it THE AMERICAN DREAM.

Our mother loved us, sacrificed for us and taught us all of the "privileges" that I believe are needed for anyone to succeed in life:

- *Belief and Faith in God;*
- *Importance of Family;*
- *Confidence in ourselves;*
- *Tough love, particularly towards me, the male child;*
- *A work ethic;*
- *Values and oversight that kept us away from the "sins" of the world, in particular, alcohol, tobacco and drugs;*
- *Putting me into Scouting (Cub Scouts, Boy Scouts—Eagle Scout, Order of the Arrow, Explorer Scouts) which introduced me to role models;*
- *Teaching me the value of learning and education.*

We lived in public housing at first. I walked to school. Our schools were racially mixed, and we took no notice because discrimination, at our age, had not been taught.

In time, a housing tract was built nearby, and my mother, a single mom, a civil service secretary, bought one. That, in itself, is the American Dream at its best.

Before I turned sixteen, I was working as a bagger at a grocery store. My responsibilities grew to include stocking and checking. Later, I worked at a fruit stand. Then I was hired full time, by Southern Pacific Railroad. I used these jobs to support myself, and later, my wife, through college. I am so grateful for my bosses who pushed me and then promoted me.

My first uniforms were in Scouting-Cub Scout, Boy Scout, Explorer Scout and the Order of the Arrow. I joined the Naval Air Reserve at 17 and attended Basic Military Training (boot camp) as soon as I graduated from high school. The military process rebuilds an individual both in ways that work to make the military effective and to build personal confidence and discipline.

I had no idea at this age that I was living the American Dream. The American Dream was not dependent on wealth or status or color. It was dependent on parent(s) that imbued their children with these values and an open society. Nor are all children raised in a loving environment where they are taught the values and behavior needed.

I admit society was not open to all citizens then, regardless of your up bringing. However, in my lifetime, the door began to open for everyone thanks to people like Martin Luther King, Caesar Chavez and many more that helped our society to unite against racism. We almost made it.

A FORMATIVE DECADE, 1963-1974

"Let the wise listen and increase in learning, and let the discerning get guidance …" (Proverbs 1:5).

"Be diligent in these matters; give yourself wholly to them, so that everyone may see your progress" (1 Timothy 4:15).

In 1963, I was 21 when I graduated from college with a degree in Philosophy. I immediately reported for duty at Officers Training School, US Air Force. During the decade of the sixties, three major disruptions happened in our society:

1. *The Civil Rights Movement;*
2. *The "Summer of Love"/Hippie Movement, which I saw as a frontal attack on our country and values; and*
3. *The Viet Nam War.*

These events, as they evolved daily, influenced me greatly.

The Viet Nam war was brutal for the American Military members and their families, but was also a proxy for the social changes occurring during the "Summer of Love." I began to believe that the "values" espoused during this revolution would become embedded in our society sometime in the future. I rejected them then and oppose them adamantly today as I see the past unfold as our future.

The individual military member during this time was hated by elements of our society. They spit on us. Called us names. Cursed us. Burned the American Flag. Refused to honor our service. They denied us credit at their stores if they knew we were members of the military. It all happened to me, personally, and I did not serve in Viet Nam, just during Viet Nam.

I did not aspire to leadership during this decade. I was just a Boy Scout determined to leave the campsite better than I found it. However, the military thrusts younger NCO's and Officers into leadership positions early. This decade tested me, formed me and conveyed and reinforced my values. "A Formative Decade" and "Role Models" also illustrate the actions of a multitude of leaders

The Civil Rights Movement

Until we moved to Biloxi, MS in 1963, we had not paid attention to the Civil Rights Movement. The South was very divided and the dissension occupied everyone's attention. We drove to Biloxi MS in a yellow Volkswagen. We stopped for gas at 11PM, still in Louisiana. The young attendant came out of the office, saw a yellow VW with CA plates and I could see the anger in his face. I got out of the car. When he saw my short haircut, he recognized that I was probably military, not an activist, and his demeanor changed.

When we arrived in Mississippi, we were confronted by a culture very different than ours on the West Coast. Schwerner, Goodman and Chaney, racial activists, were murdered and their bodies had just been discovered buried in an earthen dam in Jackson, MS. Discrimination in transportation, rest rooms, restaurants and drinking fountains was just the surface.

We rented a cottage on the Back Bay of Biloxi. Our landlords, the Lees, lived on the property and became good friends. We joined their Southern Baptist Church. The Lees were divided. Their/our church was divided. Whites did not mingle with or tolerate blacks. Southern flags were rampant. It was their fight and they did not welcome "agitators."

During our tour in Mississippi, surrounded by the Civil Rights movement, I realized I was ignorant about racism. As a couple, we were finishing college. I was working full time. I was leaving the Navy to join the Air Force. I would be gone for three months. We had to get through finals. I had a chance to test for promotion with the Navy. We were preoccupied.

I was about to grow and to change and to mature. I started, obviously, by confronting racism. We were a divided country with divided leadership. Leaders on both sides were simultaneously praised or condemned. How do you judge leadership when you have such a fundamental divide about such important issues?

Was I a racist or not? I decided the answer was no. There are absolute rules and they gave me the framework to answer the question. Faith is always sweetest when it has an application

I decided that I had to support the civil rights movement because of my Faith. Black fountains, restrooms, back of the bus? Dr. King's movement was non-violent. The white opposition used force. After we moved to Wisconsin, I visited the South several times and tried to catch up with our friends. I noted major positive changes in Southerners' attitudes towards blacks in the following decade.

Today, our society is divided through identity politics and color. The point for me is that Identity politics are opposite of Christ's commandment to "love one another." Identity politics, reparations and "wokeism" turn us into enemies of each other. This kind of confrontation will destroy this nation.

Mathew 22:37-39 ESV "... You shall love the Lord your God with all your heart and with all your soul and with all your mind.

This is the great and the first commandment. And a second is like it: you shall love your neighbor as yourself."

❖

THE VIETNAM WAR

What a disaster. We won the war but declared defeat and left in an embarrassing panic. Vietnam was a horrible icon for the changes occurring in our society then and now.

The history of conflict in Vietnam under communist rule goes back to 1949. For the United States' citizens and military, it takes legs with the Gulf of Tonkin Resolution in August, 1964, authorizing the President to take all necessary measures, including the use of armed force, against any aggressor in the conflict.

In February, 1965 President Johnson began bombing targets in Vietnam and the war was on. "Operation Rolling Thunder" followed and Marines landed near Da Nang. In July, President Johnson ordered the mobilization of 50,000 military members.

By 1971, the United States Army was in disarray. Morale deserted the ranks. Discipline disintegrated. If our citizens were not going to support the war and the fighters, why should they rot in that hell hole and die, for what? "The men themselves are fed up with the war and the draft, questioning orders, deserting, subverting, smoking marijuana, shooting heroin, stealing from their buddies, hurling racial epithets and rocks at their brothers."[4]

Saigon fell in April, 1975. 58,220 American soldiers dead. 250,000 South Vietnam soldiers dead. 1,100,000 enemy dead. 2,000,000+ civilians dead. U.S. society was deeply divided. The war, the military and its soldiers were hated.

Drugs were an accepted part of the Hippie counter culture. Society, as a whole, was more accepting of the use of drugs. So was our military. "The conflict was distinct in another way, too—over time, it came to be known as the first "pharmacological war," so called because the level of consumption of psychoactive substances by military personnel was unprecedented in American history."[5]

The Army sanctioned and provided certain kinds of drugs for our military to use. Dextroamphetamine and amphetamines were routinely issued to them without regard to the recommended dose or frequency of use. These pills substituted for sleep and fatigue and gave the soldier a sense of bravado. For short expeditions, a packet of these pills was issued to every soldier involved. Steroid injections were often used.

What could we expect? Vietnam was not a textbook war, it was guerilla war. Weak leaders, a large portion of society "hates" the war, the institutional breakdown of discipline and morale, military leaders providing drugs freely to the troops, no playbook, the soldiers were

---

4. *"Army Is Shaken by Crisis in Morale and Discipline," The New York Times, September 5, 1971, B. Drummond Ayres Jr.*

5. *The Atlantic. "Soldiers in Vietnam in 1966," April 8, 2016, Lukasz Kamienski.*

the brunt of "social" experiments and became the whipping "boys" of our society.

> *"... there were multiple reasons for widespread drug use in Vietnam: It was in part because we had the counterculture [stateside], in part because of the ready supply of the drugs, and in part because of the breakdown in morale in the Army, where a rebellion took root."*[6]

According to a 1971 report by the Department of Defense, 51 percent of the armed forces had smoked marijuana, 31 percent had used psychedelics, such as LSD, mescaline and psilocybin mushrooms, and an additional 28 percent had taken hard drugs, such as cocaine and heroin. But drug usage wasn't just limited by what enlistees could illicitly buy on the black market.[7]

Two expressions of this malaise were the atrocities committed by our own soldiers against each other ("fragging") and the atrocities committed against Vietnamese civilians. They were a result of the conditions and attitudes discussed above that were exacerbated by the rapid buildup of forces and little experience in the unscripted nature of gorilla warfare. We cranked out young inexperienced officers who became "90 day wonders." Leadership was often weak. Officers were rotated stateside every six months and enlisted troops were rotated every 12 months. Bonding and cohesion within the units was undermined.

---

6. *"The Myth of the Addicted Army: Vietnam and the Modern War on Drugs, Jeremy Kuzmarov.*

7. *History Newsletter, "G.I.s' Drug Use in Vietnam Soared—With Their Commanders' Help Adam Janos. April 18, 2018. Updated August 29, 2018.*

"Fragging." Soldiers attacked each other by using fragmentation grenades, often thrown under a tent, to kill or injure another soldier. Officers were more often the target. Between 800-1000 fragging events occurred during the war.

"The My Lai Massacre." A company of our soldiers vented by killing between 350 and 500 villagers. The victims were mainly women, children, invalids and elderly men. Gang-rapes and mutilations were part of the atrocities.

By the end of the war, the military needed to be reorganized again. The National Security Act of 1947, under General Marshall's guidance, led to a complete overhaul of the War Department. National Guard units were embedded in the Army's organizational structure intending that the Army's future mobilizations would have to include the National Guard. However, President Johnson believed that mobilizing the National Guard would turn small towns and the families of Guardsman against the war and he choose to rely on "draftees."

The damage to the military was significant. In summary:

1. *Data supplanted Leadership.*

2. *The data required, the number of dead enemy bodies in particular, would never be accurate. Think about it.*

3. *The President of the United States broke the chain of the warfighting command.*

4. *We mobilized leaving a significant and integrated fighting force, the National Guard, at home.*

5. *After the war ended, the military spent years training to integrate all of the units of the military: active, reserve and National Guard.*

6. *We used draftees which turned out to be filled with "Summer of Love" folk.*

7. *The draftees were vocal with their discontent with the war.*

A little known aftermath of the Vietnam War was the time and cost of rebuilding the military and the National Guard, in particular. I enlisted in the CA Air National Guard in 1974.

The War ended a year later. In 1979, I became the Commander of the 261st Combat Communications Squadron. We were still struggling with the aftermath of the Vietnam War. We had numerous members of the unit who were part of the social protest during the war. They hid out in the National Guard. They were disruptive and often disobedient. They dragged the morale of our units down. The military desperately needed to mend, reintegrate and to train.

In the end, we cleaned "our" house, integrated components of each branch and regained our global status as the most respected armed force on the globe. I did my part. It was not pleasant. Compliance was critical and was disregarded in very visible ways. I had the authority to issue warrants and have the Sheriff enforce the warrants through arrests. Did I? Yes.

The "Summer of Love"

What happened? The Chicken or the Egg. At this juncture in our history (the late fifties through the late sixties), the Hippie movement began in San Francisco when teens and young adults decided they did not fit in our society, they strongly supported the civil rights movement and strongly opposed the war in Vietnam. The movement spread rapidly.

They designed their own counter culture. I see them as nihilists rejecting any moral or civil authority. They were largely peaceful, but very visible. Drugs and free love were tenants of their beliefs.

Hippies expressed their opposition to our society in their events, their music, their protests, their rejection of moral authority, including laws, and in their rather vicious opposition to the military. Many left this country for Canada and other foreign ports.

Ironically, many of them wanted it both ways. President Johnson was clear that the National Guard would not face a major callup for service in Vietnam. National Guard units are based in "hometown" America. Johnson was an arrogant egotist. Calling up the Guard would awaken the "hometown." The hometown families sending their family members to Vietnam might disagree with the President. They might vote the party and him out of office if they did.

I watched society begin to mimic Hippie styles, music and tolerance for drugs; and to endorse their amoral codes of conduct. I suppose part of the allure of the Hippie culture was a shared distaste for the Vietnam War. Vietnam was an unfortunate pivoting point for the United States. I was sure that I was watching a slow-moving pivot that would affect our governance and society in the future.

A lot of this disintegration in our society was expressed, not just against the war, but more viciously expressed against the members of the military. It took a decade after Vietnam before the military began to regain public trust and respect. It took fifty years, but major tenets of the "Summer of Love," discussed above, are now embedded in our governance and in our society, as I feared then.

In 2016, Bret Stephens wrote an Op Ed for the Wall Street Journal describing this pivot and its roots in the Viet Nam War era. I was surprised anyone not living through it could see it so clearly as an historical moment in the life of our country. Here is my reply to his editorial:

February 3, 2016

RE: Bret Stephens, Op Ed, WSJ, Tuesday, February 2, 2016 Re: "Hippie Movement of the Sixties and its influence on Life and Governance Today."

Dear Bret:

You may not have lived through the sixties, but I am grateful that you understand the impact of the sixties.

I retired from the military in 1997. I enlisted in the Navy when I was seventeen. I was a young Air Force Captain during the Viet Nam War, though I did not serve in Viet Nam.

The sixties tore our social fabric. The U.S. military became a hated symbol of the attack on the traditional values of our society. I watched our senior military leadership pander to their civilian leadership and to society in shameful ways. General Westmoreland. President Johnson. Robert McNamara. Congress. The best I can say is that they were confronted with fundamental societal changes and had no choice than to deal with them. Unfortunately, they were not up to the challenge.

Johnson approved our targets daily. He refused to call up the National Guard to avoid a plebiscite on his policies. Thus, the Na-

tional Guard became a retreat and haven to those who hated the war and the military, but lacked the courage to flee to Canada. Robert McNamara ripped the guts of leadership out of the military. Body counts, General Westmoreland.

We young officers eventually had to unpack the 10 pound wigs that Congress authorized Guard and Reserve members to wear because they, Congress, did not have the courage to impose good order and military discipline during this time of changing mores.

But the point of this story is that I could see that this period would bring lasting changes to our society. These changes reinforced and were reinforced by the liberal assault on our education system that began in the early 1900s and gained traction in the 1940s. I have continued to watch this revolution unfold for many years.

So here we are as a society: dumbed down; worshipping celebrity; moral fabric in tatters; and the general electorate selling their votes for "Obama phones." There is an interesting historical note here – an inevitability: paraphrasing Professor Alexander Tyler, 1887, a democracy fails when voters discover that they can vote themselves generous gifts from the public treasury. What took them so long? Business and finance leaders, unions, the wealthy and the political elite have been exchanging votes for generous gifts for a very long time.

We are at a tipping point. While we may pull back from the brink this time, the changes in our society that began in the sixties are so deeply imbedded that I rather doubt that we can avoid falling off the cliff.

Pray that I am wrong.

ROLE MODELS

Joseph. "And now, do not be distressed and do not be angry with yourselves for selling me here, because it was to save lives that God sent me ahead of you" (Genesis 45:5).

"He who walks with wise men will be wise, but the companion of fools will suffer harm" (Proverbs 13:20).

The story of Esther demonstrates how authentic leadership is forged in intimacy with God and manifest in attention to the defenseless.[8]

8. *"Women in Scripture and Mission: Esther," Kimberly Dickson, CBE International, May 23, 2022.*

In retrospect, I got to experience and observe leadership and leaders at the very start of my career. Not all of the experiences were positive, but they were all instructive. Their acts, statements and beliefs provide me examples as they responded to the issues before them.

CDR Cecil B. Harris, a decorated WWII pilot, was my commander while I was in the Navy. He jumped in to provide personal counseling about a decision I made asking to be called to active duty early in my contract. If granted, I would have to drop out of college for two years. CDR Harris took the time to counsel me, an E1, bottom rank in the Navy. At that moment, I was the most important thing he had to deal with. It changed my life.

One day, our personnel Chief called me in. "Lotz, your contract says I have to call you to active duty soon (one year before I would graduate from college). I know you have been accepted for Air Force Officers' Training School. Will you personally guarantee me that you will swear in to the Air Force as scheduled?" Yes, Chief. He took no further action. I kept my promise. He kept his implied promise.

Their counseling provided me perspective and confidence. I graduated first in my Officer Training Class. Being a Mustang (a commissioned officer who served as an enlisted member) was important to me. I was a better leader as a result and because of the influence of the Chief and CDR Harris.

Lieutenant Colonel Don Hudgens

Col. Hudgens interviewed me for a position in the 261st Combat Communications Squadron in 1974. At the end of the interview, he offered me a position with the following condition: "John, you will be the fourth senior Captain in the 261st. The other three started their careers here as enlisted men. There are only three slots for Majors. I will try to promote all four of you, but if I cannot get all four of you promoted, the other three will be promoted. I owe them that." I wanted to serve under a leader like that. Loyalty has meaning. We all got promoted, however, I became the Commander.

That was an easy decision for me. He demonstrated his leadership in that one act. I wanted to work for Lt Col Hudgens.

Defense Secretary, Robert McNamara

A characteristic of young people, even as young adults, is that many of their early opinions on issues come from "group grope." For McNamara our collective opinion was "good manager, poor leader." We believed that our four stars "rolled" over to the President's will and lacked integrity. In retrospect, our opinions were correct. We also began to realize the importance of leadership and that leadership was different than management.

I have already described the turmoil in our society and in our military that was exacerbated, if not created, by the Vietnam war. McNamara was the Secretary of Defense-our boss. Our judgment, as junior officers, was that he was incapable of leading and was misled by his emphasis on data, efficiency and rationality, i.e., substituting management skills for leadership. Returning to the military's core leadership principles took time.

McNamara turned against the war, resigned in 1968 and is given a lot of credit for his leadership as he led the World Bank. A friend of mine lived in the Watergate and knew him. They talked about the war. Bill noted that the failure of the war in Vietnam weighed heavily on Secretary McNamara. He took to heart General LeMay's caution that we, the military chain of command, could be prosecuted as war criminals if we lost the war: Agent Orange; fraggings; drug usage enabled by military leaders; soldiers dead and disabled; deliberate massacres of civilians; and the number of civilians who were accidental casualties of war. Our managers failed to lead.

In 1995, McNamara published his book: "In Retrospect: The Tragedy and Lessons of Vietnam." He was consumed by his failures in Vietnam. He draws eleven conclusions. In my judgment, only three are relevant to his failure to lead:

1. *The failure to draw Congress and the American people into an honest and frank discussion about the war.*

2. *Not keeping the American people informed of the exigencies of a changing battlefield.*

3. *The failure to organize the leadership of the executive branch to deal effectively with the complex range of issues.*

The balance of McNamara's "lessons learned" focus on the leaderships' misunderstanding and misjudgments about the enemy, geopolitical intentions, the ability of our own leaders in the field, etc. Quite a mea culpa. While I appreciate his admission, one man put our military on the wrong path for a long time, into the mid 1980's. Possibly even longer.

The National Guard was a safe haven for dissidents who wanted to avoid being called to duty in Viet Nam. From my point of view, it took the military a decade to remove these dissidents from our ranks.

By the 1980s, McNamara's star had fallen, and not just because of his role in the Vietnam debacle. American business seemed to have lost its way, and the management methods he exemplified were being questioned. In their landmark 1980 Harvard Business Review article, "Managing Our Way to Economic Decline," Robert H. Hayes and William J. Abernathy blamed slumping U.S. fortunes on the rise of professional managers. They charged: "What has developed, in the business community as in academia, is a preoccupation with a false and shallow concept of the professional manager, a 'pseudo professional' really—an individual having no special expertise in any particular industry or technology who nevertheless can step into an unfamiliar company and run it successfully through strict application of financial controls, portfolio concepts, and a market-driven strategy."[9]

I have carried this comparison around in my files for many years, adjusting it as I gained experience. It cuts to the heart of the Management/Leadership distinction.

Manager (Boss)	Leader
Drives employees; Depends on authority; Inspires fear; Says "I"; Places Blame for any problem; Knows how it is done; Uses People; Takes credit; Commands; Says "Go!"; fails to create an environment in which his workers can succeed.	Coaches; Is Trustworthy; Generates goodwill and enthusiasm; assures his workers have the resources and training to fix the "breakdown"; mentors the workers; always gives Credit; Asks; and says "let's go!

9. *"The Harvard Business Review," Phil Rosenzweig, December, 2010.*

Conversely, however, a leader has to manage. Data and analytics, the use of state of the art equipment and tools, technology, integration of computers in the daily "business" of business are indispensable aids. They are the tools of a leader. A leader leads people, and uses tools to organize and manage the process to everyone's advantage (workers, managers, shareholders, customers).

McNamara died in 2009. "McNamara surrounded himself with young people known as "whiz kids" for their brilliance, but also their arrogance. Driven by McNamara´s quest for analytical data, they believed numbers could solve all problems." His style was so intimidating he seldom received solid and truthful feedback. He could not admit his mistakes. He believed a long war could be won by the side having the highest "kill ratios." "... dead bodies of enemy troops were counted 3-4 times, just to improve kill ratios." Unfortunately, McNamara never recognized the numbers were falsified, because he trusted numbers as "truth."[10] In a battlefield like Vietnam, it is impossible to get body counts that are accurate. So, at least here, the idea of "kill ratios" has no meaning. Perhaps the technologies of today will be game changers.

President Ronald Reagan

In 1993, President Reagan had been out of office for four years. Throughout his Presidency, I watched him lead: supply-side economics; Korbachev; The Berlin Wall; trusting and turning Paul Volcker

10. "Leadership Lessons from the Life of Robert McNamara," Bill George Blog, 2022.

loose to fight the inflation unleashed by President Nixon; tax cuts; tried to balance budgets; and so on. My regard for him grew. He was always a subject in my lectures on leadership during the last three years of my service.

President Reagan was savaged by the press. However, if you listened to what he said and observed what he did, you could see the discrepancy between reporting and reality. He had a deep knowledge of the voter and their preferences. He was a good judge of character. He knew his facts about important issues. He chose some very good advisors and trusted them. He was not a micromanager. He was inspirational. He set his own personal best interests aside. He believed in our country and trusted the voters. He wrote his own speeches on yellow, lined pads! Yet the press characterized him as lazy, old, tired and ignorant.

<u>On Humility</u>. Senator Phil Gramm tells the story of President Reagan's signing the Omnibus Budget Reconciliation Act, 1981, into law. Before it passed, thirty republicans asked for a meeting about the details of the bill. To a person, they recited their "anticipated" negative reaction to the bill by their constituencies. President Reagan's eventual response was: "<u>I have been confused. I thought this vote was about the future of our country. I didn't know it was about our political constituencies.</u>" The President left the meeting. Each of the thirty voted for the bill. Senator Gramm was a Democrat and felt the heat.

Republicans urged Senator Graham to switch parties. He decided to resign and run for re-election as a Republican. President Reagan's staff urged Graham not to resign. They believed he could not be re-elected and his conservative influence would be lost. Lee Atwater pressed the President to call Gramm and dissuade him from resigning.

The President called Atwater back. He said, "<u>Lee, the whole world does not revolve around me or my presidency. This is about Phil</u>

Gramm, and he is doing the right thing, and I can live with whatever the result turns out to be." He never called Senator Gramm. Gramm had no idea until after he resigned, ran on the Republican ticket and won.[11]

His leadership permeated everything he did as the President. In his own words:

On Perspective. "Freedom is never more than one generation away from extinction. We didn't pass it along to our children in our bloodstream. It must be fought for, protected, and handed on for them to do the same, or one day we will spend our sunset years telling our children and our children's children what it was once like in the United States where men were free."

"This is the backbone of our country: Americans helping themselves, and each other."

"I've always believed that a lot of the troubles in the world would disappear if we were talking to each other instead of about each other." 2022 redux.

"Government does not produce revenue. It consumes it."

"We've gone astray from first principles. We've lost sight of the rule that individual freedom and ingenuity are at the very core of everything that we've accomplished. Government's first duty is to protect the people, not run their lives."

On Human Nature. "A broader reading of history shows that appeasement, no matter how it is labeled, never fulfills the hopes of the appeasers."

---

11. The Wall Street Journal, August 16, 2022, Op Ed, Phil Gramm "Reagan's Lessons in Economic Leadership."

On Sense of Humor. "… the ten most dangerous words in the English language are, Hi, I'm from the Government, and I am here to help." 2022 redux.

"Prosperity is something created by people and their industries and business for which government takes credit."

On Service before self. "We make a living by what we get, we make a life by what we give. More than anything else, I want my candidacy to unify our country, to renew the American spirit and sense of purpose."

On Faith. "Each of us, each of you, is made in the most enduring, powerful image of Western civilization. We're made in the image of God, the image of God the Creator."[12]

President Reagan was one of our greatest modern leaders. It has taken too long to recognize his contributions to the success of our country.

President Obama

President Obama laid the groundwork for important changes we are seeing in our society today. For me, his terms of office were a disaster for this country. Leadership?

In 2010, President Obama's vision of America did not match the "American Dream." On October 30, 2008, he said:

---

12. *"Ronald Reagan, The Wisdom and Humor of The Great Communicator," Frederick J. Ryan, Jr., Editor, 1995.*

"We are going to have to change our conversation; we're going to have to change our traditions, our history; we're going to have to move into a different place as a nation."

He was true to his word, giving structure to what we have been witnessing since then. Today, the American Dream is under existential assault. The attempt to divide our citizens into aggrieved groups looking for reparations, and the assault on our history, standards and achievements will only enslave everyone. This assault, which I see as a continuum of social change throughout my career, has been part of my motivation to write this memoir.

Historically, we are witnessing changes today that were nascent when I first observed them during the "Summer of Love" as discussed in the Chapter "A Formative Decade, 1963-1974."

Without principled leadership, we risk losing the foundations that made us a great nation: fiscal responsibility, intellectual honesty, bipartisan debate, and, dare I say it, belief in God.

General Ronald Fogelman

As I retired in 1997, Gen Ronald Fogelman submitted a request for early retirement on 28 July 1997, one year ahead of schedule, ending his term as the Air Forces' 15th Chief of Staff. He retired early because of his disagreements with his fellow service chiefs and the Secretary of Defense over policy decisions made in the "tank," the Joint Chiefs. The issue related to President Clinton's order for General Fogelman to discharge 1st Lt Kelly Flinn and to bring charges against Brig Gen "Terry" Schwalier in the aftermath of the Khobar Towers bombing.[13]

General Ronald Fogelman was appointed the Chief of Staff of the United States Air Force in 1993. He released a statement of core values for the Air Force that year. They continue to provide guidance today, and they immediately resonated with myself and later with my grandson when he was introduced to them in Air Force Basic Military Training.

"Integrity first. Service Before Self. Excellence in all that we do."

Fogelman's Core Values still resonate with me. I have tried to live by them, and more. We are humans, so I will not claim perfection in that process, but I recognized their importance intuitively as I continued to grow as a person and as a leader. These core principles inform and guide me every day.

General Fogelman was presented with an ethical dilemma. General Fogelman's early retirement was an act of courage, conviction and upheld the ethical underpinning of leadership. He epitomized the core values he wrote. His decision to resign early rather than be forced to exercise an unjust command from the President of the United States repudiated the actions of President Johnson, Secretary McNamara and the Four Stars during the beginning of my military career.

Thank you, General Fogelman. I still regret not accepting your invitation to join you and our class at "Charm School" for the BBQ and evening playing foosball at your home.

---

13. *"Loyal Dissent: "General Fogelman and the Decision to Retire Early." Jonathan M. Slinkard.*

CHRIST

Who Humbled Himself. He gave us a new commandment that can make a huge difference in our relationships with each other and without which you cannot lead.

He exemplified servant leadership over 2,000 years before a book on servant leadership became the new standard in 1970:

> *…"If anyone would be first, he must be last of all and servant of all" (Mark 9:35).*
>
> *"… that you love on another: just as I have loved you, you also are to love one another" (John 13:34).*

I call it tough love, and that is what He practiced. His teaching provides a framework for all of our judgments.

FUNDAMENTALS OF LEADERSHIP

*"Let the wise hear and add to their learning,
and let the discerning get guidance" (Proverbs 1:5).*

*"Do nothing from selfish ambition or conceit, but in humility
count others more significant than yourselves" (Philippians 2:3).*

*"Not many of you should become teachers, my brothers,
for you know that we who teach will be judged
with greater strictness" (James 3:1).*

INTRODUCTION

The opportunity to lead is a gift. Becoming a leader is a life-long learning process. Be aware of influences in your life that may guide you as you step into a leadership role. Prepare yourself to succeed. Study leadership to increase an understanding of your role. Genuinely redefine yourself as your experience leads you. Be prepared for failure. Learn from it and turn failure into a positive experience.

Life probably offers everyone opportunities to lead, for a moment or for a lifetime. When you land in your first position of leadership, you are handed a remarkable gift. For me, the purpose and satisfaction for the leader is to become a role model and to mentor others. Wade in. Learn. Be humble, seek advice and admit it when you stumble. You need a big "leadership tool bag" to find the best tool for any particular situation that you encounter. Start identifying and gathering those tools early in your career.

Leading is contextual. Growth as a leader will be defined one experience, one traumatic event (or more) and one observation at a time.

Never stop studying and learning. A journey is ahead. Understanding this "art form" called leadership, depends on your commitment to becoming a student of the subject. Know the goal of the leader, the principles and roles of leadership and understand your personal characteristics (both those that are helpful and those to be avoided) and core values, i.e., your qualities.

As you study leadership, begin to identify your personal limitations, hopefully, before those limitations trip you up. I rarely exhibit anger, but occasionally, I do. In those instances, I can only walk away since I have learned that success flees the moment anger is present. So that becomes an unwanted characteristic of mine that I try to avoid. And remember:

Key leadership themes are presented below to provide a basic outline of the subject of leadership. Studies of the great achievements of "great" leaders are uplifting, motivating and instructive. However, leading is first about helping those in your organization to accomplish more humble goals as they themselves are given the opportunity to grow and to succeed. You are their mentor and your achievements are measured by your success as a mentor.

I suggest there are five types of leaders:

1. *Those who accomplish amazing feats to achieve amazing results- "Big Hairy Audacious Goals" (BHAGs). They are the ones likely to inspire a book.*
2. *The selfless, servant leader.*
3. *The ignorant, uninformed and accidental leader.*
4. *The self-serving leader, which may be an oxymoron.*
5. *A "leader" motivated to achieve genuinely evil purposes.*

❖

PRINCIPLES OF LEADERSHIP

As we talk about the Principles of leadership, I remind you that "... the line dividing. good from evil ..." runs through our hearts (Aleksandr Solzhenitsyn). Leaders can lead from either side The implied premise of Leadership Studies is that Leaders pursue virtuous goals and work for the general benefit of their organizations and of mankind. Think about it.

A principle is an immutable rule, truth or a standard that is fundamental to behavior or to how things work. It is a basic truth or proposition serving as a foundation for a system of beliefs. They come with the job. They should be learned, understood and applied. They are based on the experience of generations as they see certain principles that consistently work over long periods of time. They become universal. A leader must be genuine in everything they model.

- *Create a shared Vision.*
- *Lead by example.*
- *Model Excellence.*
- *Embrace innovation and change.*
- *Take Aristotle's Advice on page 60.*
- *Communicate.*
- *Admit your mistakes; forgive other's.*
- *Integrity required.*

- *Laser focus on the objective. Only success counts.*
- *"Check Six," that is be aware of your blind side. For a pilot the blind side is the rear of the aircraft. Change may be hiding there ready to bury you.*
- *Listen.*
- *Kaizen (Continuous Improvement)*
- *"The Buck stops here."*

ROLES

There are specific roles that are exclusively the responsibility of the leader:

Organize to "Achieve Influence." The leader has to "achieve influence" within his or her organization. Maxwell's assertion sounds self-seeking. However, earning the confidence of the organization requires that one of a leaders' first personal goals has to be to insure that the members of the organization have a path for their own growth and success. It takes a team.

Leaders need to create a Constructive Environment. This foundation is described in the "Nicomachean Ethics." Aristotle concludes that: "The role of the leader is to create the environment in which all members of an organization have the opportunity to realize their own potential." This foundation is the basis needed to "achieve influence."

It also lays the foundation for the team to achieve the organizations' goals. It is not the role of the leader to create an environment to enhance his or her own power or ego, but to create an environment in which everyone can achieve their potential by being united and while focused on the organizations' goals.

"Vision"-Purpose. An organization is built around a vision or purpose. The goal is to make it clear to the team what the organization is and what the mission is. A vision statement has to be based on a realistic assessment of the organization and its capabilities. The leader should articulate the vision. However, many organizations' vision statements are the product of a team. This role will be discussed in more detail below under SWOT. Without clarity of purpose, the organization fails, and:

"Without vision, the people perish" (Proverbs 29:18).

Build a Culture. Elements include values, standards of conduct, work styles, courtesies, styles of communication, dress, equity, respect for each other, and so on.

Rules of Conduct. This is an area where a leader should consult key people in the organization. The rules cannot discriminate. The final decision is the leader's. It is important that the rules are clear, fair and that they are consistently and fairly enforced.

Enforcement and Arbitration of the Rules of Conduct. The leader's role. Subordinates may carry out the enforcement, but there must be clarity that the leader was the final voice approving the enforcement process.

Observes and assures praise that is earned, is recognized in public and assures that discipline required is swiftly carried out in private. There can be no favorites.

Sets and enforces standards. Especially, hold senior leaders responsible for failures.

Builds the Business Strategy and Monitors all results: the team, waypoints and financial impacts. Clearly defines the market (segmentation) and competitive differentiation.

Communication. He or she "works" for the employees, the board of directors, the vendors, bankers and the customers. Employees need to know how they, individually, the teams and the organization is doing.

Develop Leaders within their organization. The Marines in battle callout "... next man up" when the squad leader is killed or wounded. There must be 1-3 other members of the squad trained to step into the Squad leader's role immediately.

Go to the Fight. Never ignore problems. Deal with them now.

Manage Risk, Opportunities and Change.

SERVANT LEADERSHIP

This concept has gained popularity relatively recently (1970). It was a huge variation on how we looked at leaders. Ironically, this principle is Biblical and was modeled and taught by Christ over 2,000 years ago.

Leaders are often identified by the rank or title they have: President, Manager, Captain, General, Crew Chief. Too often "leaders," euphorically, use their title or rank simply to tell their people what they will do to accomplish the objectives of the leader and of the organization. The "leaders" see themselves at the top of the pyramid that defines their organization, society or team. The "leaders" are normally empowered with the authority to discipline, to promote, to demote, to hire and to fire members of their organization.

Servant Leadership was introduced in 1970 by Robert Greenleaf.[14] A little late, but a great wake up call. The Apostle Mark nailed the idea about one thousand nine hundred and forty years earlier as he walked with Christ.

> *..."If anyone would be first, he must be last of all and servant of all" (Mark 9:35).*
>
> *"The greatest among you shall be your servant. ... whoever humbles himself will be exalted" (Mathew 23:11).*

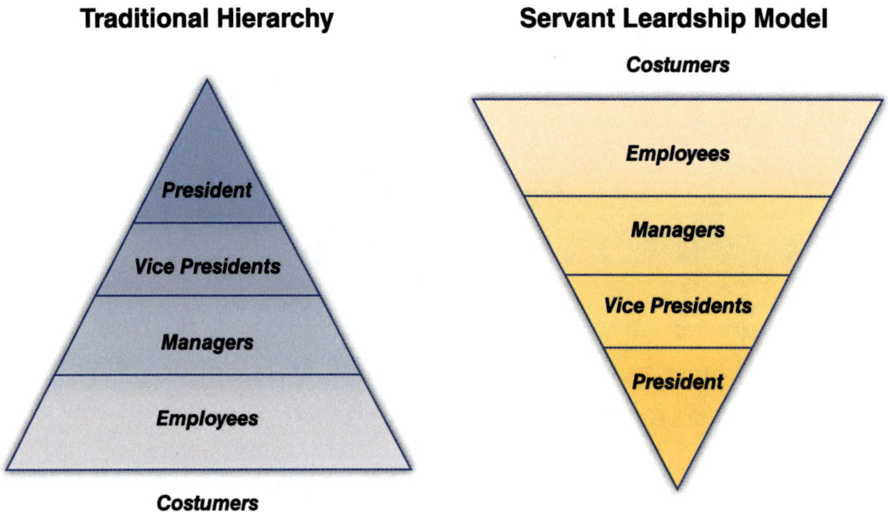

---

14. "Servant Leadership," Robert Greenleaf, Paulist Press, 1977.

The normal pyramid on the left suggest the President is more important than the customer in that the authority and power emanate from the CEO and flow to the bottom. More importantly, the point Greenleaf makes is that a leader must share power with those led and first be concerned about mentoring his or her employees so they learn, grow and succeed within their organization.

The value of this illustration is to point out that the organization is responsible, first, to customers, then, in sequence, to all elements of the organization that serve the customer. It does not mean that the leader is not in charge or that he or she will not ultimately be held responsible for the organization's success or failure. But it focuses on the team nature of leading an organization. One person at the top cannot succeed without mobilizing those that work for him or her which means creating an environment where they grow and succeed together.

Servant leadership is an attitude, not a call to work alongside subordinates. As a Colonel I was the warfighting commander of a Combat Communications Group. Our mission and training involved setting up heavy communication vans to create a communications system on remote mountain tops.

Putting rank aside, I would often help the troops set up ten-man tents. Then one day, one of my Chiefs came up to me and whispered: Colonel, you need to go do Colonel things and we will do NCO things. What a lesson in leadership even though I thought I knew better than to fraternize with my troops!

As I weave through my personal growth and lessons in the next section, it gets messy. That is what leading can look like. Leading will demonstrate the rather unpredictable dynamic you will encounter. Every situation encountered in leading has elements that may be similar, and probably as many that are unique to the specific situation.

What is the leader's reward: money, power, recognition, adoration? I do not think we have to worry about the leader's reward. A successful servant leader will receive everything that is due because he or she mobilized the team, created a path for them to succeed, and the organization succeeded.

LEADER'S CRUCIBLE

The authors below have written extensively about what makes a great leader. I recommend their books and this article. In this Article, they asked: "Why is it that certain people seem to naturally inspire confidence, loyalty, and hard work, while others (who may have just as much vision and smarts) stumble, again and again?"[15] They interviewed forty executives over three years.

In this round of interviews, they found evidence that stratifies leaders. Those leaders that "… endured intense, often traumatic, experiences that transformed them and became the source of their distinctive leadership abilities."

This "crucible" event, was defined as "adaptive capacity," i.e., "… the ability to transcend adversity and become stronger in the end …" "It's composed of two primary qualities: the ability to grasp context,

15. Harvard Business Review on "Developing Leaders," Warren G. Bennis and Robert J. Thomas article "Crucibles of Leadership."

and hardiness." The ability to grasp context implies an ability to weigh a welter of factors, ranging from how very different groups of people will interpret a gesture to being able to put a situation in perspective. Hardiness is the "perseverance and toughness" to move through very tough encounters as you lead.

In my notes on leadership dated October 2, 1992, at the age of 51, I wrote: "It's apparent from this vantage point that you cannot be wise unless you have suffered, made mistakes and endured failure. I have and can say that the journey has been difficult. Unfortunately, I am not sure I have obtained wisdom. I at least understand that the "obtaining" is not an end state, but a process." I concluded saying, "Consequently, the final judgment will be made by others, and only after my death."

Born or Made

Studying and defining leadership is not a science. We can define elements of the subject, but the combination of issues that one leader will face in a lifetime are infinite and unique. There are infinite combinations of important leadership characteristics as well. Every leader will bring a unique combination of their characteristics to apply to a unique set of issues.

I believe that there are core characteristics that you either have or can acquire or are hidden within you that you discover as you mature. There are personal characteristics that lead both to success and to failure. However, while a few characteristics seem essential, our confirmation comes from examining the lives of leaders and trying to understand how they lead successfully and what characteristics they brought to the fight.

I believe that some of our personal characteristics lie dormant. We may not be aware of them. After all, how many leaders are students of leadership at the beginning of their adult lives. I began to understand myself and my leadership potential only as I led. Then, I became more attentive to the notion of "leadership." I began to pull up and examine numerous issues to learn about leadership. I did not articulate certain characteristics like "servant leadership" until it was popularized. Yet looking back, I realized that I intuitively understood and applied the principle very early in my adult life. When I was promoted to Captain, I got my crew together and thanked them. I said: "I got promoted because I had the privilege of standing on very tall shoulders-yours." While I meant every word, I also recognized that getting promoted to Captain is pretty routine.

KNOW YOURSELF

Do not run away from a leadership role because you do not think you are a leader. Looks, deep voice, poise, etc. are non-starters. Take some time to take the inventory discussed below and to try to apply it to yourself. However, If you do not like people and lack integrity, do not aspire to lead.

Who Are You? Know yourself. Certain personal characteristics are anathema to being a leader. Conversely, you may not appreciate or have discovered characteristics you have that may make you a great leader.

If you are a complainer and always critical, self-centered, cup half empty, pessimistic and you believe that people are generally inferior to you, do not even try to lead. Your attitude will be discovered quickly and people will not follow you. If you succeed to a leadership position, you are likely to damage your organization for years to come.

Are you articulate and good looking? No points. It does not matter.

If you care for people, respect them and have a positive attitude towards them; if you are a person of integrity; are confidant, but not arrogant; are able to delegate and give credit and praise; you possess essential characteristics needed to lead. There are more characteristics, however, the reality is that any recognized leader may not have some of the characteristics that we value.

Personality traits have consequences. Are you optimistic? You will convey your optimism. Are you forgiving? If you are, you heal. Can you let go? If so, you grow. Are you a person of integrity? If not, no one will follow you. Do you believe in the inherent goodness of people? Trust? It is most often self-fulfilling. Selfless? You will be respected. Humble, but confident? You will reap respect. Do you tackle your problems-go to the fight? Trouble, suffering and failures increase your fortitude as you learn from them.

As you start the journey and move into even the most humble leadership position, you may or may not have any role models or understanding of your new role. However, begin to observe other leaders at any level. Note their qualities and styles. Try to discern the principles they espouse and take notes. Leading can be akin to trial under fire. Persevere.

> *"Suffering produces endurance, and endurance produces character, and character produces hope and hope is not an illusion" (Romans 5:3-4).*

TOOLS FOR LEADERS

SWOT (Strengths, Weaknesses, Opportunities, Threats). Most large organizations seem to have a vision statement. A vision, a goal or a purpose is meant to provide a clear direction for the organization. Sometimes, the vision statement contains a brief comment about the ethics of the organization or supports moral benefits for society.

If an organization is serious about the benefits of a vision statement, it should lead to an actionable plan based on an analysis of the organizations' strengths and weaknesses.

Our military's purpose is to protect and defend the citizens of this country and to protect its resources. We write "Ops Plans" starting with a goal (vision or purpose) such as "Win the war in Germany." Great. How? The Ops Plan that evolves gets into specific objectives, unit assignments, phasing, etc., and it assesses weaknesses and strengths, and adds contingency plans accordingly.

SWOT is a comprehensive tool. It starts with an assessment of Strengths, Weaknesses, Opportunities and Threats (SWOT). A SWOT assessment is tedious, but it has multiple benefits:

1. *Organizational assessment;*
2. *Setting a Vision (direction);*
3. *Establishing Goals to reach the vision, and breaking them down to Objectives with teams assigned to meet the objective within a time frame.*

I have led or participated in these sessions more than once.

In civilian life, it is more subtle. This whole process gets rather fuzzy, in my opinion. Is the vision statement the leader's sole responsibility (yes, I say) or is it the job of the committee undertaking the SWOT analysis (no, I say)? A consensus "vision" has no soul, no ownership. If the leader of the organization can envision BHAGs (Big, Hairy, Audacious, Goals) for the organization, he or she will excite the workers.

A vision statement has to be motivational and attainable. I favor one that challenges an organization to stretch, to overcome difficult obstacles or to do something never done before. Create a vision statement that is motivational and attainable. In the end the you have to sort these questions out. Here are some samples to suggest the differences in Visions, i.e., Goals. Which resonate with you?

Apple: "To make the best products on earth, and to leave the world better than we found it."

Tesla: "To create the most compelling car company of the 21st century by driving the world's transition to electric vehicles."

ABYSSE: "Produce less, produce well."

United By Blue: "A world without waste."

Nike: "Do everything possible to expand human potential."

Make-A-Wish: "That people everywhere will share the power of a wish."

President John F. Kennedy said:

"We choose to go to the moon. We choose to go to the moon in this decade and do the other things, not because they are easy, but because they are hard, because that goal will serve to organize and measure the best of our energies and skills, because that challenge is one that we are willing to accept, one we are unwilling to postpone, and one which we intend to win, and the others, too."

Our pastor wrote this Vision Statement for our church: "Worship Jesus; Love One Another; and Serve the World."

SWOT, or any assessment of an organization, is not complete until an action plan is written with assignments and completion dates. The Vision/Mission statement, i.e., the organizations' goals or purpose, follow the organizational analysis, but precede writing the Operations Plan that sets forth objectives, time lines and assigns people to achieve the objectives.

ONE MAN'S JOURNEY

"Do nothing from selfish ambition or conceit, but in humility count others more significant than yourselves" (Philippians 2:3).

"Not many of you should become teachers, my brothers, for you know that we who teach will be judged with greater strictness" (James 3:1).

"As in water, face reflects face, so the heart of man reflects the man" (Proverbs 28:7).

"Better is a poor man who walks in his integrity than a rich man who is crooked in his ways" (Proverbs 28:6).

Putting It All Together

Life is repetitive.

Human nature marches on, likely not changed over generations. "Nothing new under the sun"? Ancestral wisdom passed down as proverbs, cultural values and common sense are a simple way of expressing well-known truths or adages based on common sense or experience, i.e., lessons learned and passed on for generations. They become part of societies' traditions.

Yet very generation encounters its "own" sets of problems to solve. Perhaps the "sets of problems" never really change at their core. The proven wisdom of the past continues to be forwarded to new generations, as noted above.

United or divided, I believe that society continues to need principled leaders who are trustworthy, guided by a servant's heart, and who seek to help, uplift and unite those within their spheres of influence. The open-ended dynamic of leading is you, the leader, the person. Every leader is a unique person bringing different characteristics and core values to the table.

Every generations' leaders have to mobilize the creative energy of the members of their team(s) in order to win. The win could be a war. It could be satisfied customers. It could be to achieve the Big Hairy Audacious Goals (BHAGS) of true visionaries who have no existing model for their bold leap forward. It could be to save souls.

Writer and philosopher Ralph Waldo Emerson once said,

> *"Our chief want is someone who will inspire us to be what we know we could be." In one brief statement, Emerson sums up the importance of leadership and how leaders can help others achieve great things. Leadership isn't about holding authority over someone else. It's about positively influencing people to reach new heights.*[16]

Again, I encourage you to take up the leadership gauntlet even knowing that you may not move the master dials at all. First, however, make sure you have a servant's heart. If your goal is to be a leader, I believe you will fail. If your goal is to serve others, I believe that you will succeed. I rejoice that I had the privilege to lead, and I pray that I touched lives in a positive way. Leading changed and improved my life and my being.

Pathways

I am thankful that I started my military career in the enlisted ranks. I am grateful for having done manual labor early in my life. These

16. LEADERS, "Leadership Important," Colin Baker, Updated September 7, 2022.

experiences first taught me the dignity of work. They taught me that you really don't know what you are doing at the beginning and that I had a lot to learn.

Leading in the military and in civilian life have significantly different paths and outcomes. The military awards rank that vests authority, and defines levels of responsibility, to very junior people. You are the "boss" in a way not seen in civilian life.

A turning point comes when you realize you are now part of the "Profession of Arms." The outcomes are different for military personnel. People can die. In the Army and Marine Corp, enlisted members are the "pointy end of the spear." They die first. In aviation, the officers are the "pointy end of the spear," and they die first.

Military members, and first responders across the board-fire, police, medics, rescue teams, etc., commit our individual services to others understanding that the consequences are truly significant.

Gaining Influence

Practicing leadership can be very subjective and fuzzy. It is a form of art requiring infinite variations tailored to each situation. The goal of leadership is to gain influence with those led. The purpose of gaining influence is to achieve the goals of your organization. Sounds simple, however, you do not step into a leadership role and inherit influence. It has to be earned.

To gain influence, the leader should start with Aristotle's advice: "... create an environment in which all members of [the] organization have the opportunity to realize their own potential." You have to create a positive and motivating environment in the organization so that everyone has the opportunity to succeed. I am not talking about "Completion Certificates" or vapid cheerleading, I am talking about motivating and mentoring through tough love.

Never forget that those you lead know more than you about the organization than you know. You need them more than they need you. If those you lead like and respect you as a leader, and if you have created the environment Aristotle suggests above, they will help you. If not …

Core Values

Core Values are learned and adopted, not genetic. They become our internal compass that helps guide decisions, actions and purpose. Core values determine whether you can lead successfully, or not. Elvis Presley was quoted, apocryphally, as saying: "Values are like fingerprints. Nobody's are the same, but you leave 'em all over everything you do."

> *"Let love be genuine. Abhor evil. Hold fast to what is good. Love one another with brotherly affection. Outdo one another in showing honor. Do not be slothful in zeal. Be fervent in spirit. Serve the Lord. Rejoice in hope be patient in tribulation be constant in prayer. Contribute to the needs of the saints and seek to show hospitality" (Romans 12:9-13).*

The organization will know by your words and works whether you are genuine. Stick to your values to the very best of your ability.

Core values make a huge difference. Some values are taught early in your life. It took time for me to sort out my core values. They are:

- *The Faith that I live by.*
- *Caring for others and understanding that Tough Love is an essential part of genuine caring. Caring is an order of magnitude deeper than mere friendship*
- *Being a person of Integrity. Am I trustworthy and accountable? Fair and objective?*
- *Selfless. A Servant Leader.*
- *Leave the campsite better than you found it.*
- *Time is of the essence. Use it wisely.*
- *Courage. Will you go to the fight? Deal with problems now? Administer tough love? Have you been tested? If not, do not be surprised if you fail. Make sure you understand what the "fight" means within your sphere of influence.*
- *I value learning thanks to my grandmother who was my role model.*

Characteristics of Leaders

Characteristics are notable individual qualities or properties that distinguish one person from another. Our personal characteristics are instinctive or learned but become baked in, and, in time, they define us. They are an important part of our personal ability to lead. I suppose there are both genetic characteristics, and that we can adopt characteristics.

Lists of characteristics can be very long, duplicative and very impractical as useful guidance. Some characteristics listed are not essential for leaders to possess. I have seen lists with 4-500 characteristics.

The military may be an easier context to define a leader's essential characteristics. Combat units' success or failure can win or lose wars, cause a nation to be subjugated and save or lose thousands or millions of lives, both military and civilian.

Civilian organizations have important goals and missions to perform that benefit the owners, workers and society. Success or failure is measurable and important to the members of the organization and to those they serve. This environment probably permits a broader range and mix of leadership characteristics.

Over many years, I have developed my own list of the essential characteristics of leaders. On February 7, 1993 I wrote: "I believe there are certain ineffable qualities possessed by people who might be commonly identified as leaders." My list of characteristics and values included:

a. Faith.

b. A genuine regard for the well-being of other people embedded with Tough Love.

c. Integrity and intellectual honesty.

d. Selflessness/Service before self.

e. Humility.

f. Courage.

g. Reliable.

h. Authentic.

i. A student. Intellectual capacity and curiosity.

j. *Optimistic, enthusiastic.*

k. *Self-confidence cushioned by intellectual honesty.*

l. *A capacity for work—energy.*

m. *Vision and perspective.*

n. *Impatience [but] with understanding.*

o. *Fairness and objectivity.*

p. *Sense of humor.*

q. *An understanding of, but not necessarily an acceptance of, human frailties.*

r. *Cheerful*

s. *Adaptable*

Here is a partial report card on my character weaknesses. I hope it is instructive and encouraging. No one is perfect and no one is safe from the intrusion of evil in our lives.

a. *Integrity and intellectual honesty are essential. It is my oath to my family, friends and the organizations that I serve. Everyone trips, however, including myself. Each stumble has made me stronger and more aware.*

b. *Serving others, service before self, has become an essential part of who I am. Fairly early in my military career, I realized that I could never live with myself if I watched someone in physical trouble or being assaulted without intervening. At this stage of my life, my commitment is to serve others through my faith and for my family and friends. Mentoring is a form of serving others.*

c. *Sympathetic. Yes, if it is deserved. "Tough love" is an act of sympathy and caring.*

d. *I am optimistic, most of the time. But I am a realist and continually test my optimism. I do not want my optimism to be based on false premises. I am slightly manic/depressive, so my moods vary, sometimes undermining my optimism.*

e. *I am self-confident, sometimes to a fault. I am a Type A personality. Pilots also have a consistent psychological profile that includes a high degree of self-confidence.*

f. *I have always had a high capacity for work. To a fault. I have had employees come to me, literally in tears, saying they can't keep up with me. I was not trying to be a role model in this regard. That is who I am. I was not trying to impose my work standards on my employees. The episode was a useful learning moment suggesting I pay closer attention to my employees and their comfort and morale. I became more human, more connected.*

g. *You have to have a high regard (love) for individuals tempered by the willingness to administer "tough love." This theme has taken me time to sort out and to adopt. I am critical and I could not reconcile my regard for individuals with my condemnation of human beings generically. My problem was my failure to segregate the really bad people and everyone else.*

h. *Intellectual capacity and curiosity are essential. Others will have to judge me on those characteristics.*

i. *Courageous, yes. However, I am not sure that I have been adequately tested. I am frank and have been characterized as being a critical person. In my defense, you cannot leave the campsite better, or help people grow if you are blind to things that need to be fixed. The leader has to do the heavy lifting. They have to make judgments. They have to deal with objections. They have to administer "tough love."*

j. *I like the view from 30,000 feet better than being mired in detail. Vision is the ability to see ahead and imagine where opportunities or obstacles might exist, or when or where change is a benefit or threat. Perspective is the ability to see relationships and interrelationships. My personality gravitates naturally to the big picture. Perspective, for me, was largely a matter of gaining experience.*

k. *Impatience, particularly in today's environment, may be a disability. On the other hand, information, ideas and competition move at an incredible pace given technology. Impatience motivates creative thinking. But haste can "make waste."*

l. *Fairness and Objectivity are critically important. It undermines the leader if he or she fails. However, the perception of others in the organization may judge you either way depending on their bias or prejudice towards issues on the table or towards you. I believe that I have done well in this area.*

m. *A sense of humor is essential. You get what you give. It can lift people up. It can ease tension. I also understand that not everyone has a sense of humor.*

n. *Human frailties exist in all of us. You are the mentor, the teacher and the judge. You set the standards and create the environment. Not everyone is going to fit entirely in your organization or warm to you personally. Be objective.*

o. *Embrace change. I have an initial tendency to bring skepticism to the table and first to "test" the change. Most features of our lives have some basis in tradition. Generations have given us certain rules of conduct and frameworks for passing judgments. Change may be inevitable, but change is not always beneficial for society, the collective "we" or the organizations we lead. Change is disruptive.*

Inventory your strengths and weaknesses. My "confession" above conveys the message that leaders are not perfect. We should admit our negative characteristics and build safe guards. You may not be able to eliminate some undesirable characteristics.

No matter how you rank in core values and characteristics, brick walls exist. They include:

1. *The intransigency of human nature;*
2. *There are degrees of evil in all of our hearts; and,*
3. *Egos consistently get in the way of leading.*

Growth as a leader will be defined one experience, one event, and one observation at a time and all within a unique context. When you are young and inexperienced, your best job will be one where your boss is a leader. Most of us start to learn leadership by emulating our bosses.

Deal Breakers

Essential Characteristics and Core Values, which I call Leadership Qualities, define us, individually, to those that we lead. They are our personal variables unlike the Roles and Principles of Leadership that stand on their own and that should be understood, adopted and practiced by all leaders.

Leaders will reflect different mixes of qualities. Qualities have to fit the person. In spite of the many lists that exist, I believe that there are three Qualities leaders must have to lead. They are:

1. *Willingness to put Service Before Self;*
2. *Integrity; and,*
3. *Tough Love.*

You can succeed as a leader without checking all of The Qualities boxes, however, without genuine Tough Love for others, Integrity and Selflessness (Servant attitude) you cannot lead. People will not follow you. Part of the power of these Qualities is that they link naturally to other important characteristics, values and principles. They "Bloom" as I will illustrate below.

Selfless Leadership

Selfless Leadership is an attitude that may be natural, or can be adopted. It presents a challenge for a leader. A leader at any level, gets more attention, pay, perks, access to peer leaders, to bosses and to customers. It is easy for ego to get in the way. Then a leader starts looking up more than looking around and down.

You build your reputation from the bottom up, and more importantly, by standing on the shoulders of those you lead. You cannot jump onto their shoulders, you have to be lifted up by them.

It may sound cynical that you have to gain influence with those you lead. However, your genuine commitment to their growth and well being opens those doors. This is a team "sport." They are the team, you are the coach. Those you lead, you mentor in an environment that enables them to grow and to succeed. Your integrity and tough love foster trust, and confidence that you are helping them to grow and to succeed.

The Book of Mathew starts with a criticism of the Gentiles and high officials:

"Jesus called them together and said, the rulers of the Gentiles lord it over them and their high officials exercise authority over them" (Mathew 20:25).

This is an explicit judgment against that style of leadership exhibited by the Gentiles and high officials saying instead:

"Not so with you. Instead, whoever wants to become great among you must be your servant,..." (Mathew 20:26).

When a leader puts his or her personal interests and ego gratification behind the needs of those led, trust has a footing, integrity can be tested, and the door opens for real team work.

"One of the outstanding ironies of history is the utter disregard of ranks and titles in the final judgment men pass on each other. The final estimate of men shows that history cares not an iota for the rank or title a man has borne, or the office he has held, but only the quality of his deeds and the character of his mind and heart." [17]

Appearance does not count. Being in charge does not mean you are leading. Information, analysis, data and running the numbers are only dumb tools. They help the leader make decisions. Just remember:

"Certainly we cannot serve others until we have taken charge of ourselves; we cannot teach what we do not know ..." [18]

---

17. *Samuel Brengle, Salvation Army-Research.*

18. *William Barclay, "The New Daily Study Bible, The Letters to the Corinthians," 1975.*

"… If anyone would be first, he must be last of all and servant of all" (Mark 9:35).

"The greatest among you shall be your servant … whoever humbles himself will be exalted" (Mathew 23:11).

"… let the greatest among you become as the youngest, and the leader as one who serves" (Luke 22: 26-27).

Selfless "Blooms"

❖

Selflessness is also a characteristic evident when the leader loves others. It starts with a genuine regard for the well-being of those led, a Selfless attitude. Never forget the corollary though: tough love. Selfless Leadership requires a leader to demonstrate integrity and to be trustworthy.

Integrity

❖

The Air Force Motto is: "Integrity First. Service Before Self. Excellence in everything we do." General Fogelman, 1993.

Being a person of Integrity is a tough standard. Integrity is the foundation of trust. It speaks to intellectual honesty. Credit is given where it is due. On the one hand, it is likely impossible to act with integrity without some failure. We may be able to lead, but perfection is not within reach.

Yes, we all fail from time to time. When you lead, you are under a microscope. Some people will look for a crack in your armor to give them an excuse to defy you, or, perhaps, just to feel assured that you are a human being after all. So, all we can do is to be aware and to try our best to exhibit Integrity in every matter relevant to our life and make it a natural part of our leadership.

Integrity "Blooms"

The flip side of the integrity coin says: Trustworthy. Integrity is key to other qualities such as intellectual honesty and that is closely related to moral courage, fairness and objectivity.

Tough Love

> *"A new commandment I give you, that you love one another: just as I have loved you, also love one another" (John 13:34).*

William Barclay notes, in his Commentary on the Book of Romans:

> *"Love must be completely sincere. There must be no hypocrisy, no play-acting, no ulterior motive. Christian love is cleansed of self; it is a pure outgoing of the heart to others."*[19]

19. *"The New Daily Study Bible, The Letter to the Romans," William Barclay, 2002, Westminster John Knox Press.*

I do not believe that you can lead people without "loving them." However, Christ's version of love is tough love. He will call you to task and admonish you.

Your troops will not follow you to and through the battles ahead without it. They are prepared because of it. It will bond you and those you lead because the tough love assures those you lead that you are training them for success. After all, in the military, a leaders' order may result in a persons' death. I assure you that "loving" is not mushy and was not modeled in the "Summer of Love." But that was not love, anyway.

Our children are now taught that everyone gets a "participation" trophy and that leaders are only "cheerleaders." Discipline is not permitted since it implies failure and that is not permitted, we cannot be judgmental. Nonsense. Our children will fail. Society will fail. There is no reconciliation between these two versions of "love."

Loving and reproving are emotional opposites. Your "love" returns "love." Your "reproach" may return anger towards you. Nonetheless, loving and reproving those loved represent an absolutely necessary continuum.

The continuum of tough love includes praise for real success, recognition, awards and more. The continuum also includes disciplining, correcting, training, firing, putting folks on probation, setting standards, enforcing standards-the tough and emotionally draining stuff. You cannot lead if you shy away from the "tough love."

"Whoever spares the rod hates his son, but he who loves him is diligent to discipline him" (Proverbs 13:24).

"Those whom I love, I reprove ..." (Revelation 3:19).

The leader has to believe people are inherently good. This love spectrum, considering the diversity and complexity of people, is very tough on a leader. You will be whipsawed by the ensuing emotional dramas. Loving will test your confidence in your leadership, without mercy.

"My son, do not despise the LORD's discipline or be weary of his reproof, for the Lord reproves him whom he loves, as a father reproves the son in whom he delights" (Proverbs, 3:11).

"For the Lord disciplines the one he loves, and chastises every son whom he receives" (Hebrews 12:6).

Your successes will energize you, but come with an emotional cost. You need to keep an emotional safe place for yourself. As a leader, you cannot become a close friend with those you lead. Keep some distance.

At the Harvard Business School, they show the film "Twelve O'Clock High" in courses on leadership. The current commander of the unit has gotten too close to his airmen and is emotionally devasted by the high death toll in the unit. His emotional state clouds his failure to require his airmen meet the highest flying and tactical standards required of a "top gun."

Gregory Peck comes in to replace the existing commander. He initiates a stand down. He finishes his assessment and begins a very tough retraining regime and restores discipline to the unit. He demands high standards. The unit begins to succeed again. The death toll drops dramatically. The enemy is dying, not his troops. Then the emotional stress gets to Peck, and he begins to move into the emotional morass that caused the other commander to fail. Leading is not for the faint of heart.

Tough Love "Blooms"

Its Qualities include Selflessness, Objectivity, Trustworthiness, Honesty, Sympathy, Courage, and Generosity.

THE ART OF LEADING

You have to be yourself as a leader. Be careful to check your ego and to present yourself as you are. Focus on your team to insure even the slug (See Sun Tzu in the "Art of War") on your team is productive and has a chance to succeed.

Listen

Shape Conversations. Communicating starts by being a good listener, as well as presenting your thoughts with clarity. Make sure you are understood. Conversely, when listening, make sure you understand. Listen more than talking. You have to live by your core values and your distinctive characteristics. They have to be genuine. Failure to lead by example, even once, can cause your failure.

"The General would like …" Beware. "The General, i.e., the leader, would like …" are words usually uttered by a subordinate wanting to enhance his or her standing with both his or her peers and with the general. I fault the general. He or she is talking, not listening.

Too many times a leader, the "general," calls a meeting of subordinates and fails to frame the discussion or to be quiet and to listen.

> *"Whoever keeps his mouth and his tongue keeps himself out of trouble. Scoffer is the name of the arrogant, haughty man" (Proverbs 21:23-24).*

Define problems, ask for solutions, listen and give credit. Overall, your employees know more about the organization than their leader, particularly the broken parts, worker tension, inefficiencies, theft, morale and more. An arrogant leader who displays anger or impatience, who fails to acknowledge good input, who shows distain, who closes his or her door to workers creates a negative environment which will undermine a leaders need to "gain influence."

Venues for communicating create learning experiences for your employees. They gain comfort and confidence as they participate in constructive meetings or get opportunities to interface directly with their leader. If they have been blessed to work for a really good leader, they are watching and mimicking as the leader mentors.

Be careful. Do not think "out loud" in front of subordinates. They want to please you. On occasion, I would find out that an NCO or junior officer heard me say something, largely to myself, and without intending to launch a project, only to find out in a couple of weeks that the "project I requested" is underway.

So, remember, leaders cannot be naïve in their dealings with people. If leaders do not understand and parry human nature ..., trouble lies ahead. Humans are self-centered and they can be manipulative. Listen; speak discretely; and let your example convey your message. The people in your organization know what's going on collectively.

So gain influence. It is a team sport. Create the environment for them to use their knowledge to establish content, direction and priorities within your framework.

Title and Rank

When first promoted to General, we attended "Charm School" for two weeks. Certain themes were pounded in during every discussion:

1. *A general officer (leader) lives in a fish bowl. Everyone can see what you are doing.*
2. *Don't gloat or preen or act in a way to denigrate the office you hold.*
3. *Keep quiet and listen. You will never have all of the answers, much less the know all of the questions to ask.*

"Rank is a tool that is matched to the job you have been asked to do. Without the proper title, you may not succeed in your new job." My boss, Maj Gen Tandy Bozeman, Adjutant General, CA National Guard, articulated this thought when he was promoting one of our officers to Brigadier General. Wise counsel. Stay focused on the job at hand, not who you are or your rank. Be grateful, not boastful.

You Get What You Give

What a remarkable insight. What can you can get by first giving? This insight is a gateway to leading by example. I have taught my grandchildren continuously the idea that "you get what you give," a paraphrase of Matthew 7:12. Think about it. What do you bring to the table that opens doors, opens hearts and minds and that teaches by example every day? What can you first "give" and what is returned?

- *A smile will beget a smile.*
- *A quiet voice is heard and answered quietly.*
- *Optimism is contagious and lifts everyone. Give it and it returns immediately.*
- *Are you forgiving? You will have it returned to you.*
- *Can you let it go? Give it away? Humility usually wins over ego.*
- *Are you a person of integrity? If not, no one will follow you. If you are, trust binds, teaches and lifts everyone.*
- *Do you believe in the inherent and dominant goodness of people? Pass it on. Change someone's life forever*
- *Energy energizes.*

"So whatever you wish that others would do to you, do also to them ..." (Matthew 7:12).

Good and Evil

Leaders lead by gaining influence. Virtue struggles with our weaknesses, particularly ego and the "evil" part of our nature. I would hope that a leader always leads his or her people for their own benefit, as well as for the organizations' benefit. The first begets the second. A skeptic might call it manipulation.

As we talk about the Characteristics of Leaders, remember that … the line dividing good from evil … runs through our hearts. Leaders can lead from either side of that line. The implied premise of Leadership Studies is that Leaders pursue virtuous goals and work for the general benefit of their organizations and of mankind. However, even revered leaders have clay feet and can succumb. Be diligent and humble.

Our personal characteristics are instinctive or learned but become inherent in us and they define us. Arguably, they are the most important part of our personal ability to lead.

We seem to ignore the question of genuine evil and how to characterize evil with respect to "leaders." Generally, evil is not included in discussions about leadership. Are we content to say that these people are leaders even when pursuing evil visions? We can probably agree what kinds of acts, goals, lead us to call a "leader" evil.

I have introduced a panoply of leaders that influenced me. I listed leaders that both inspired me positively and negatively, and I have stated my case. However, at the extremes, I believe that genuine evil does take over. The true goals and visions of an "evil leader," are disguised, and a "higher" goal is espoused that justify acts that are horrific. The real beneficiaries are those leaders themselves, not the people they serve. Are they leaders as meant in most books or studies about leaders and leadership?

At the extremes, few would dispute categorizing Hitler, Mussolini and all of worlds' most vicious dictators with evil and self-serving intent. I believe that truly evil leaders have and do now exist, and have existed throughout history. My judgment is that if evil is the leader's goal, that there is no leadership. What are the characteristics that brought them so much "success," though short lived? A leader and righteous objectives have to be linked. Enough.

- *Ecclesiastes 8:11 "... the heart of the children of man is fully set to do evil."*
- *Proverbs 28:7 "As in water, face reflects face, so the heart of man reflects the man."*
- *Proverbs 28:6 "Better is a poor man who walks in his integrity than a rich man who is crooked in his ways."*
- *Solzhenitsyn: "... the line dividing good and evil cuts through the heart of every human being.* [20]

"KISS IT"

Flatten Your Organization. Complexity is expensive and slows progress. Decentralize and flatten your organizational structure along with decision making authority. That also means assuring that the subordinates keep the "monkey," i.e. the problems assigned to the employee, on their backs. When subordinates come to you for advice the monkey is on their back, however, their goal is to leave that responsibility (the monkey) in your office. If they leave a meeting with you and are happy, look around your office to insure they have not simply transferred the monkey to you, the boss, rather than taking your advice on how to solve their problem - the monkey.

---

20. Gulag Archipelago, Published 1973.

Personal Rules to Lead By

When interacting with people, these personal insights about yourself and your Environ-ment are basic elements for establishing relations with people, in this case, people you lead. Integrate these characteristics and insights. They speak for themselves. Be genuine or risk being discovered. Trust will be destroyed and any claim about being a leader with integrity will be undermined.

- *You swim in a fish bowl. Everyone sees what you are doing. Leave your ego in the office. You have the title, the office and the authority. Your people know it:*
- *Keep your personal life personal. You need a sanctuary.*
- *Be willing to admit your mistakes, and make sure there is tolerance for mistakes at all levels. The balance, of course, is that there is a limit on tolerance for repeating the same mistakes.*
- *Know your core values. You are being watched. Model them. Then create common core values within your organization-something simple and with bite that reflect your core values.*
- *Boy Scouts are taught to "Leave the campsite better than you found it." The Japanese say "Kaizen." A corollary is to embrace change that improves what you do. Change can also be very disruptive depending on the frequency and magnitude.*
- *Leading an organization is a Team Sport. Every role in an organization is filled by an important person since every role is, by definition, important to the organization's success.*
- *Keep your distance. No favorites. Particularly involving anyone in a leadership role. Favoritism destroys your credibility and their trust. Do not fraternize.*

- *When you have to counsel a member of your team, start the session with a summary of what he or she is performing well, then describe the problem needing attention and try to help the person develop solutions and the resources required.*

Anchors.[21]

Lessons learned, generally, the hard way: I blew it. We are far from perfect beings and we will stumble. I call them "my anchors" because this is how I try to live, and I know I will fail and will need to know where to go when I do. The first one keeps me focused and grounded. It keeps me humble, and that is no mean feat.

⚓ *My role in life is to serve, protect and defend my Faith, Family, Friends and Country. That is my focus and my grounding. I will continue to dedicate my search for ways, daily, in which I can carry out that vision. I will go to the fight.*

⚓ *Face the tough issues first and "go to the fight"-now.*

⚓ *We are taught to take care of our people. We cannot be taught to care for people. If you don't like people, don't try to fool them. You will be discovered. Your leadership will be rejected and fail.*

⚓ *The best of the leaders that I have observed in my career have risen because they have been able to bring the best out in the people who work for them.*

⚓ *The best of the leaders are coaches, mentors and cheerleaders to and for the organization. They permit people to make mistakes while assuring that they aren't repeated.*

21. My notes since 1969.

- ⚓ *Judging Character. "Gresham's Law" (Bad money drives out good) applies to Humans. First, understand the frailty of humans. Understand that human nature doesn't change easily. It doesn't matter why a person is tainted, i.e., bad. Your good reputation is not likely to improve another person's bad reputation. However, their bad reputation will be more likely to degrade your reputation by virtue of the association.*

  I choose to accept people the first time we meet. No judgment. I don't know them, but until I do, I have no reason to reject them. I cannot judge them (Christ's summation of the law). Everyone is hiding a dark side and some evil intent. In the end, I can choose not to socialize with them, however.

- ⚓ *"Check Six." The enemy's assault will come from your back, the six o'clock position that you cannot see. Make "Check Six" a byword.*
- ⚓ *I was a Boy Scout. Be Prepared. Leave the campsite better than you found it. Kaizen it.*
- ⚓ *Don't forget that entropy is a one-way street. Nature is moving towards homeostasis, a state of equilibrium between independent elements, relentlessly. You can slow it but you cannot stop it.*
- ⚓ *"The secret of success is constancy of purpose." Disraeli.*
- ⚓ *Successful Leaders Stand on Tall Shoulders.*

Role Modeling

A leader has to do his or her best to be role models. Leaders are human. We all have our Achilles' Heel. If you have been led well, be forgiving when you discover this failure in the leader(s) you admire, self-assess and move on.

"You cannot lead by memo or email. You cannot lead by shouting, berating or demeaning others. You cannot lead by abdicating your responsibilities and pointing fingers at others. You must lead by example!"[22]

Statements of values define the characteristics of the organization. I encourage organizations to make their values clear: the customers are always right; service to the customer is first and foremost; we recognize the value of our workers and respect their beliefs; courtesy to all; "Integrity first. Service before Self. Excellence in everything we do," could be examples of statements of values. But they do not point the organization itself in any direction at all, i.e., goals for the organization.

Finessing Your Role

- *Set high standards of conduct and expectations for the organization.*
- *Enforce the standards consistently. Praise, in public, when it is deserved. Discipline, in private, when it is deserved.*
- *Train and evaluate continuously.*
- *Have a system to reconcile grievances and disagreements.*
- *Permit mistakes, but not repeats.*
- *Never sweep issues under the rug, particularly if they involve senior leaders.*

---

22. E.P. Unum, Essay.

- *Discipline Yourself and Your Workers.*
- *Create an Environment for Success.*
- *Sun Tzu in "The Art of War" warns the General that every organization has a slug in it. It is the General's responsibility to find a place in the organization where even the slug can succeed.*
- *Make sure your people know that you value them and their contributions to the organization and to yourself, personally, large and small.*
- *Give them the freedom to fail and to learn.*
- *Accountability for a failure should include their ability to articulate why they failed; take corrective actions; and to avoid a second failure.*
- *Deliberate or malicious acts that undermine the organization will not be tolerated. Follow the rules, or advocate for their change, or leave. The organization is hurt otherwise.*
- *Demonstrate that your first priority is to support the organization/team and that transgressions that weaken the team (its members) will not be tolerated.*
- *Be clear that you will be the toughest on the leaders in the organization. Carry it out.*

The leader has to be somewhat detached from those they lead. A leader cannot be their buddy. The love of and respect for others that are essential characteristics of a leader, require tough love as discussed earlier. Know and Respect Your People. They know what is going on.

In 1 Corinthians 9:22, Paul says: "I have become all things to all people, that by all means I might save some." Paul is not is not being disingenuous. He is simply saying, I owe people the courtesy of getting to know them, regardless of who they are, before I can lead them, in his case, to Faith.

Do not ever feel that you have to have all of the answers. You won't even know the right questions to ask most of the time. But the "organization" knows. Listen first. Engage your other workers and become informed by them.

There is no silver bullet. Leaders are individuals and possess all of the flaws of those they will lead. However, I am convinced that no one should even attempt to lead if they cannot pass the "love and respect people" test.

If you have the authority and are a leader, use it with humility. If you are arrogant in your authority, you will undermine or destroy your leadership. Leaders, lead, and serve their organizations. They espouse and expect certain standards of those who work for them. You are being watched continuously. Do not carve out exceptions for yourself or for "favorites" (it is hard not to have favorites, but everyone knows) or for senior leadership.

A dilemma for a leader is that the leader is responsible to "someone else," and to the people in the organization they lead. "Someone else" may call important shots and may be a terrible leader. "Someone else" may not like people. The people, themselves, are flawed yet can make or break the leader. The leaders' success and self-esteem are at risk. The leader may feel conflicts of interest towards the people in the organization and "someone else." The terrain can be very difficult to navigate.

My Personal Rules of Conduct

It is important to know those you lead. Problem solving, progress reviews, walking around observing and being accessible, open-door policy, disciplining, meetings, socializing... However, I think it is important to keep a certain amount of distance. You have to be objective. Favoritism is hard to conceal and it is devastating to morale. These are my personal rules along with some priority courtesies I observe:

- *Keep your personal life private.*
- *If you have the authority and are a leader, use it with humility. If you are arrogant in your authority, you will undermine or destroy your own leadership role.*
- *Leave the party early, the employees will appreciate your understanding.*
- *Never interview the other sex without another person present.*
- *Never go to the head of the line irrespective of your rank.*
- *Never ask your people to go out in the rain unless it is really important.*
- *Never go to sleep until you are sure all of your people have a place to sleep.*
- *Insecurity is easily discovered, and so is false confidence.*
- *Be real, be yourself and be comfortable in your own skin.*
- *If you are not comfortable, there are times when you can confess it and solicit other input.*
- *You will have to give direction and issue orders and override some opinions, Get over it.*
- *Promote diversity within the natural limits God has created. Be fair at all times.*
- *Brutal honesty is sometimes required. Don't make brutal honesty the first thrust if avoidable.*
- *Celebrate success and give proper credit for it.*

Proverbs 15:1 "A soft answer turns away wrath, but a harsh word stirs up anger."

Proverbs 16:21 "… and sweetness of speech increases persuasiveness …"

A CALL TO SERVICE

"What has been is what will be, and what has been done is what will be done and there is nothing new under the sun" (Ecclesiastes 1:9).

"Leadership matters. But the old way has run its course. Leadership today must be based on purpose, inspiration, caring and compassion." [23]

---

23. Raj Sisodia, Babson College, Professor of Marketing.

Today, as Yogi Berra was fond of saying: it is "deja vue, all over again." Human nature does not change, dooming us to cycles that repeat predictably. The United States is again in a state of crisis and needs leaders who will honor their oath of office and who will serve their constituents without personal aspirations.

As I ended my military career our citizens had been split into multiples of groups according to color, economic status, sex, sexual "preference" denying sexuality at birth and more. Since then, we have been exposed to junk social theory and rewritten history like DEI, CRT and "1619." Each group identified is deemed to have suffered unique discrimination deserving reparations and they are coached to feel threatened by other groups who are also taught to compete for "the largesse."

Too many leaders have again prostituted themselves for rank, power, wealth and they stand with others who have espoused, and are willing to implement, the changes that will destroy the United States of America and its Republican form of government as articulated in the Constitution of the United States, 1787. The same comments and failure to adhere to their oath of office applies to our political leaders.

One thing is absolutely certain:

> *"The rise of woke politics has undermined public confidence in the brass. The current era is marked by fading trust in U.S. institutions, but confidence in one pillar has held up: the military. But now, even that is eroding and the question is whether the brass will get the message. Some 62% said "military leadership becoming overly*

> *politicized" reduced their confidence some or a great deal. Some 52% also had reduced confidence in uniformed officers. Half cited "so-called 'woke' practices undermining military effectiveness."* [24]

As I see it, this cycle of civil disobedience had roots in the late 1950s culminating in 1968. It laid the foundations for what we are experiencing today. Campus riots are deliberate acts of civilian disobedience organized which are subsidized by notable families and infiltrated by professional rioters.

"All of this shows that the spreading protest movement isn't a political accident. It's part of a larger strategy of spreading disorder to force colleges and U.S. policy to bend to the left's will and demands. As events this week at Columbia and UCLA show, trying to appease this law-breaking will encourage more of it. The students are pawns."[25] "So it really is 1968 all over again ..."[26]

A substantial number of leaders today are pursuing personal goals that are not beneficial to the citizens or the country.

> *"Do not expect the radical left to survey the wreckage of socialism and communism in history and accept that statism impoverishes people and erodes their freedoms. There will never be admissions by our elite that progressivism exists mainly for the acquisition of power by the utopian and virtue-signaling few, who ensure that*

---

24. The Wall Street Journal, *"Americans are Losing Trust in the Military," November, 2022.*

25. The Wall Street Journal, *"Rules for Campus Radicals, 2024," Editorial, May 3, 2024.*

26. The Wall Street Journal, *"Cookie-Cutter Campaign Protests," Daniel Henninger, May 9, 2004.*

> *they are never subject to the baleful implementation of their ideological agendas on the rest of us."*[27]

The United States, and all the good that it stands for, currently faces an existential crisis. We have opened our public treasury to support ruinous policies. The voter has access to the treasury. We are literally buying and selling votes. Alexander Tyler and Thomas Jefferson have warned us.

I noted that Tyler suggested that "The average age of the world's greatest civilizations from the beginning of history, has been 200 years.[28]

By 2010, President Obama's vision of America did not match the American Dream. On October 30, 2008, he said, as often quoted by his wife Michelle:

> *"We are going to have to change our conversation; we're going to have to change our traditions, our history; we're going to have to move into a different place as a nation."*

The flaws and weaknesses imbedded in our democracy were articulated very early in our history. More simply and bluntly: "The American Republic will endure until the day Congress discovers that it can bribe the public with the public's money."[29]

---

27. "American Greatness," Victor Davis Hanson, June 10, 2024.

28. Alexander Tyler, 1887, "The fall of the Athenian Republic," Scottish Professor of History at the University of Edinburgh.

29. Attribution Uncertain. Alexis de Tocqueville.

Finally, Thomas Jefferson penned warnings to future generations about the vigilance required to maintain our liberties under the new Constitution that the founders wrote. His warnings bring us to the time in which we live as society is torn by these very issues:

"The democracy will cease to exist when you take away from those who are willing to work and give to those who would not."

"It is incumbent on every generation to pay its own debts as it goes. A principle which if acted on would save one-half the wars of the world."

"I predict future happiness for Americans if they can prevent the government from wasting the labors of the people under the pretense of taking care of them."

"My reading of history convinces me that most bad government results from too much government."

"The tree of liberty must be refreshed from time to time with the blood of patriots and tyrants."

"To compel a man to subsidize with his taxes the propagation of ideas which he disbelieves and abhors is sinful and tyrannical."

CLOSING VIGNETTES

"Let us make mankind in our image, in our likeness, so that they may rule" (Genesis 1:26).

"Each of you should use whatever gift you have received to serve others, as faithful stewards of God's grace in its various forms" (1 Peter 4:1).

"For even the Son of Man came not to be served but to serve, and to give His life as a ransom for many" (Mark 10:45).

Yes, leave your ego behind and put your rank aside. However, your team will still respect your rank. There are certain "perks" and courtesies that are bestowed with rank. They will expect you to take advantage of them. They know that you have specific responsibilities that no one else can perform. They know that proper executive "perks" are given to make the leader more effective-to clear the desk of "menial" tasks.

Be sure to find time to leave your desk or your office to visit and talk to your team. Observe what they do. Listen and question as you go. They want to see you and to talk to you. Get to know them and identify those with potential. Leaders need continuously to identify leadership potential and mentor it. Depth of leadership is important, particularly in the military as previously discussed.

I have illustrated Secretary McNamara's complete focus on gathering data to use to manage outcomes. His failure, illustrated during the Vietnam War, haunted him for the rest of his life. Managers devise and manage processes. They are the people who direct the activity of their "employees." If data is the driver, there seems to be little room for the expression of creative, motivated intelligence except to follow the data and use the processes in place. Data is a tool, not a principle.

2,500 years ago, Sun Tzu said: "The General must be possessed of wisdom, honesty, benevolence, courage and discipline."[30] Sun Tzu identifies essential characteristics that a General must have. The framework is war and the significance is its outcome. It takes leadership to win a war. Without those characteristics, Sun Tzu implies that the General can't lead and will not win.

Leading is hard work physically and emotionally, but it is rewarding in spite of the bouts of frustration and self-doubt. You have to make the hard decisions. Sometimes you have bad news for your team. Failure always looms. When you win, they get the praise. When you lose, simply take the blame. Whether you are ever acknowledged for your role, I trust you will find your own peace and pleasure taking this journey.

Love one another. Share with one another. Help each other. Don't avoid issues. Be timely in your intervention. Walk the talk, i.e., be genuine. Go to the fight. We are dependent on each other. In our life time, we need to help and uplift each other. Time is precious. We only have today. So take up the leadership gauntlet. You will have served those you led. The process will be your reward.

As I interface with the people in my life, I rejoice that I had the privilege to lead, and I pray that I touched lives in a positive way to help them and to make their life more meaningful, successful and loving.

---

30. "The Art of War, Sun Tzu, Chartwell Books, Inc., Michael Spilling, Editor.

The best leaders that I have observed in my career have been able to bring the best out in the people who work for them. They create an environment in which people can succeed, and they manage to focus that energy of the organization towards a single goal or direction that is commonly understood. They are willing to admit their own mistakes. They take care of their people, firmly, as necessary. They challenge people to higher standards of performance and they set and enforce unequivocal standards of behavior. These people lead by example; they are visible and manage by "walking and talking."

I once heard someone say that: "People are any organization's most important balance sheet asset even though they are not listed on the balance sheet. They leave at night and you should pray they return in the morning. If they do return, rejoice." As a friend often pointed out: they come with a brain at no extra cost. People have great intelligence and common sense. The challenge to managers and leaders is to create an environment which taps into these resources and allow people to succeed. People should be treated with respect and given the maximum responsibility and authority. They should expect integrity and loyalty from their leaders and should be expected to reciprocate.

People will fail. Failures and mistakes should be expected in a dynamic organization. The only real failures are to stop trying, to fail to admit mistakes, or to fail to learn from mistakes. When properly motivated, there is no limit to what people can achieve. We should continuously expect more of ourselves and our people.

Military leaders, in particular, should be selfless and completely focused on the mission and the troops. Our positions [titles], our rank and our perquisites represent a temporary trust, a tool, not a right!

Life may be a fluke. It doesn't matter. Human nature speaks to the issue. We all have family and dear friends that we love, socialize with and would help in most dire circumstances. Acts of kindness, protection, help, encouragement are imbued in our hearts. Why?

I believe that leading makes you a better person. Make your life count. Live it in confidence for the right reasons. Never Fear. God will always set you on the right track if you ask and are willing to yield.

About the Author

JOHN M. LOTZ

Brigadier General, USAF, Retired

General Lotz was reared in Riverside, Calif., and graduated from La Habra High School in 1959. He received a bachelor's degree in philosophy from California State University, Long Beach, in 1963, and went on to earn his master's degree in business administration from the Harvard Business School in 1971. His professional military education includes completion of Squadron Officers School, 1976; Air Command and Staff College, 1979; and the National Security Management Course, 1981.

Enlisting in the Naval Air Reserve in 1959, General Lotz served as an air traffic controller while attending college, attaining the rank of petty officer third class in the U S Naval Reserve. He enlisted in the U.S. Air Force to attend Officer Training School, Lackland AFB, Texas, and was commissioned a second lieutenant upon graduation in 1963. He graduated first in his class. He then completed the ground electronics officer course at Keesler AFB. Miss., and accepted a regular Air Force commission in December 1964.

He was assigned to Truax Field, Wisc., as officer-in-charge, Systems Quality Control, Chicago Air Defense Sector. He then performed duty as a guidance control officer in the Thor missile program at Vandenberg AFB. Calif. and Johnston Island, in the Pacific, attaining the rank of captain, before resuming civilian life. General Lotz continued service in the active Reserves until 1974, when he was appointed as a captain in the California ANG. At that time, he was assigned to the 261st Combat Communications Squadron, in Van Nuys, as a communications-electronics staff officer. He went on to become chief of maintenance, and then commander in 1979. In 1981, he assumed command of the 234th Combat Communications Squadron in Hayward, and in 1982, was appointed deputy commander of the 162nd Combat Communications Group, located in North Highlands. In 1989, he assumed command of the 162nd CCG, and in 1990, was appointed to his present position at the state headquarters.

His military decorations and awards include the Meritorious Service Medal with one bronze oak leaf cluster, Air Force Commendation Medal, Air Force Outstanding Unit Award with two bronze oak leaf clusters, Air Force Organizational Excellence Award, Combat Readiness Medal with one bronze oak leaf cluster, National Defense Service Medal with one bronze star, Air Force Longevity Service Award Ribbon with one silver and one bronze oak leaf clusters, Armed Forces Reserve Medal, the Small Arms Expert Marksmanship Ribbon, and the Air Force Training Ribbon and the Legion of Merit. California state awards include the Meritorious Unit Citation, California Service Medal with one device; State Service Ribbon, and Drill Attendance Ribbon with three silver stars.

In his civilian capacity, General Lotz is the managing general partner of Bay Ridge, Inc. a land development company in Monterey, Calif., and is a director of the Monterey County Bank and the Affordable Housing Corporation.

His civic affiliations include being the past director and president of the Monterey Peninsula Chamber of Commerce and Visitor and Convention Bureau and is a past director of the Private Industry Council. He is also a member of the Harvard Business School Alumni Association of N. Calif., the National Guard Association of Calif., and the U.S., the Urban Land Institute, and the Chamber of Commerce. An active civilian pilot, he holds a commercial pilot's license with single and multi-engine land, instrument, and helicopter flight privileges. He holds an FAA certification as a flight instructor, including an instrument flying instructor rating.

The general was promoted to and federally recognized as a brigadier general on April 8, 1992.

General Lotz left active Air Force duty in 1969 to attend the Harvard Business School. When he graduated in 1971, he was hired by a NYSE Company as the Vice President, Corporate development. He spent twelve years working on acquisitions and as the Vice President and General Manager of four of the company's divisions. During this period, he was a member of the Air Force Reserve and then joined the CA Air National Guard in 1974.

In 1983, he financed and purchased the land development division of the company spending twenty three years as a developer and builder and later as the CEO of a bank's real estate division. He retired from business in 2011 after also acquiring a giftware manufacturing company and building a full service aviation Fixed Based Operation.

During his career, he has served on numerous boards of directors including thirty five years on bank boards. Since 2011, he has been involved part time in Merger and Acquistion brokerage, aviation consulting and is a member of several boards of directors.